Le Thoronet Abbey

A Cistercian Abbey

In 1098, Robert de Molesme founded a "new monastery", a reformed Benedictine abbey, at Cîteaux near Dijon. When Bernard de Fontaine—the future Saint Bernard—arrived several years later, the order began to expand. Cîteaux and its first four "daughters"—La Ferté, Pontigny, Clairvaux and Morimond—grew quickly. All these abbeys were linked together by the *Carta caritatis,* a code of statutes defining the rights and duties uniting the "mother abbey" to the "daughter abbeys". The Cistercians pursued a strict application of the Rule of Saint Benedict, written in the sixth century, which stressed the importance of a balance between manual work and prayer, and of a remote location in which to pursue their chosen life-style. Saint Bernard was one of the first theologians to propose a philosophy based on the relationship between art and salvation, although

Aerial view of the abbey, set in a forested valley in the back country of the Var region.

he did not impose a specific model. He did not banish artistic creation, but instead recommended a pure art which had no embellishment or bright colors, along with an aesthetic that integrated volume, light and beautiful stone carving. The aim of this austere harmony was to help the monks internalise their faith. This artistic vision was clearly at odds with that of the Benedictines of Cluny, who glorified God through the use of luxurious materials and ornate decoration.

The abbey of Le Thoronet, nestled in a valley amid a forest of oak trees, but near arable land, represents a perfect example of this ideal. Its architecture is characterised by a simple, functional beauty; the design itself reflects the theological and artistic concerns of the order.

Yet Provence was not one of the usual areas chosen by the Cistercians, who founded only six abbeys in this region in the twelfth century. Le Thoronet, Sénanque (Vaucluse) and Silvacane (Bouches-du-Rhône), known as the "Three Sisters of Provence", still retain interesting architectural elements, but only ruins remain of the three others—Valsainte, Silvacane's daughter abbey (Alpes-de-Haute-Provence), Ulmet and Silveréal (Bouches-du-Rhône), which were built later and were far less prosperous. In the thirteenth century, female religious communities founded several new establishments: Notre-Dame-du-Plan

The abbey viewed from Darboussière hill, 1962.

Le Thoronet and the Cistercian convents

The amazing surge in spirituality which inspired the creation of so many monasteries in the twelfth century was also decisive to the development of convents during the thirteenth century. Many of these convents were drawn to the Cistercian rule. When the Premonstrants would no longer accept women, the Cistercians welcomed them. This was one of the modern features of the order, although the chapter remained fundamentally hostile to women, who were held responsible for original sin. The nuns were subject to a severe rule of conduct; they were obliged to remain cloistered (although they did not always abide by this rule), but above all, the convents had to have enough funds to remain self-sufficient. Most of the female communities in Provence already existed before they became affiliated with the Cistercian order. The abbot of Le Thoronet, who held the spiritual and temporal administration of Saint-Pons-de-Gémenos and of Notre-Dame-de-Sion, did not create these institutions. He was, however, supposed to visit them on a regular basis. He usually delegated this task to one of his monks, who acted as a confessor and chaplain, as well as bursar. The relationship between the convents, their lay protector and the ecclesiastic guardians (the abbots and bishops) was often characterised by conflict.

Saint-Pons-de-Gémenos convent, 1971.

The women abided by the rule of the order, which was, however, somewhat adapted to their specific needs (codifications of 1237 and 1257). The nuns also adopted and maintained the principles governing the architectural concepts and organisation unique to the order: the few remaining churches are remarkable for the purity of their architecture. Current research demonstrates that specific arrangements—the installation of galleries in the church and the separation between the priests' choir and that of the nuns, for example—were also made.

(Vaucluse) and Saint-Pons-de-Gémenos (Bouches-du-Rhône), the only one which still exists; the daughter abbeys of Mollégès (Bouches-du-Rhône), Saint-Pierre-de-l'Almanarre (Var) and Notre-Dame-de-Sion in Marseille; and the priory of Notre-Dame-de-Beaulieu in Arles, which was under the guardianship of Mollégès. The history of Saint-Pierre-en-Demueyes (Var) is unclear: it appears that this small community of women, linked to Le Thoronet in the mid-fourteenth century, was never officially incorporated into the Cistercian order.

HISTORY

The Initial Community at Notre-Dame-de-Florièges

The abbey of Mazan, situated in the Vivarais, was a daughter abbey to Bonnevaux in the Dauphiné (a province of ancient France), and therefore a "granddaughter" of Cîteaux. This abbey founded Notre-Dame-de-Florièges—or Florieyes, named after the nearby river—in the township of Tourtour (Var). The document recording its creation is dated 14 April 1136, although its context is obscure. In 1140, Raimond and Étiennette des Baux signed an act donating salt marshes and pastures, but it was the count of Provence, Raymond Béranger II, who, in 1147, ratified the property of the abbey of Florièges after quelling a revolt by the Provençal lords led by Raimond des Baux

himself. The ratification took place in the presence of Boniface de Castellane, the local lord who had rallied to the count. The founder of the abbey is unknown, because very few archives have survived, and also because little is actually known about the region's history during this period.

Furthermore, we know nothing about the material and spiritual lives of the first monks. According to legend, the body of Guillaume, a monk at Florièges considered to be a saint by his peers, was placed in the tomb that is now located in the eastern arcade of the cloisters of Le Thoronet. Saint Bernard himself is said to have brought a reliquary from Rome to house the forearm of the deceased monk.

Transfer to Le Thoronet

The monks did not stay long in Florièges, probably because the arid, windy site was ill-suited to the Cistercians' agrarian system. Monks moved from place to place far more often than is generally believed. The Florièges community thus moved to Le Thoronet, some twenty-five kilometres to the south, and settled on land which they already owned. The exact date of this move, which probably occurred in 1157, is not known. The monks maintained certain buildings at Florièges which were linked to their pastoral activities. A chapel, built after the abbey was founded, still remains, along with a few ruins, which were incorporated into the buildings of a farm in the nineteenth century.

The valley selected for the present-day abbey was less remote than the previous site, but it had several advantages: it was close to fertile fields and it had several streams and a plentiful spring. The origin of Le Thoronet's name may, in fact, be derived from the pre-Latin root word *tol,* meaning 'spring'.

A Prosperous Abbey

The entire abbey was constructed at the same time, which explains the exceptional architectural unity. It was probably well

The former abbey of Florièges is now part of a farm building, 1992.

underway by 1176, the year in which the abbey's properties were once again ratified by the count of Provence. Most historians date the church to the third quarter of the twelfth century. The other monastery buildings were constructed throughout the following century. This chronology remains rather uncertain, however, due to the lack of documentary sources and any serious architectural study of the site.

Proposed extensions to the abbey were never made, probably because of limited funds. It did not expand, and attempts to incorporate other abbeys failed. In 1199, the abbot of Le Thoronet was punished by the general chapter for trying to bring an abbey into the order, an undertaking that was considered to be too risky. Several years later, the abbey asked the general chapter, in vain, for authorisation to incorporate a community of canons located on Porquerolles Island. Le Thoronet was, however, responsible for the souls and the property of the female religious communities in the region. By the late thirteenth century, there were no more than twenty-five monks at the abbey. The fact that some of these abbots were appointed to Episcopal sees in Marseille, Sisteron and even Toulouse seems to indicate, if not the moral stature of these men, at least their involvement in the social and religious life of the region.

Donations continued to flow into the abbey through the mid-thirteenth century, allowing it to continue its farming and animal-breeding activities. The abbey acquired a vast expanse of landed property, a fact that created some conflict with neighbouring religious establishments, such as the Benedictines of La Celle. Unfortunately, it is hard to determine the exact extent and nature of this property, as most of the medieval archives have disappeared over the centuries. Summaries of the old deeds, made in the sixteenth and eighteenth centuries, do not portray a clear picture of the realities of medieval life. The location of the granges—monastic buildings maintained by lay brothers on land situated far from the abbey—has been particularly hard to determine. During the thirteenth century, the Benedictine monastery of Correns

Folquet de Marseille

Folquet de Marseille, son of a merchant from Genoa, was probably born in 1150. This troubadour was famous in his time and left behind some two dozen songs written from 1180 to 1195 in a highly sophisticated style, several of which are lovely works on religious themes.

In 1195, while the courtly world of his youth was changing, he abandoned earthly affairs and retired with his family to a Cistercian monastery—some historians have suggested, erroneously, the Grandselve monastery, located in the Tarn-et-Garonne. Elected abbot of Le Thoronet in 1199, then Bishop of Toulouse in 1205, he became personally implicated in the Albigensian crusades starting in 1209, and actively supported the preaching of Saint Dominic. He died in 1231 and was buried in the Grandselve abbey.

Less than one century later, Dante placed him in "Paradise", where, he said, this "jewel . . . luscious and costly" of Venus's sky shone "like the choicest ruby stricken by the sun" (Canto IX, *The Divine Comedy,* translated by Hendy F. Cary, New York, Collier).

Folquet de Marseille, bishop of Toulouse (French manuscript 12473, Paris, Bibliothèque nationale de France).

7

transferred the chapel of Saint-Croix, located along the banks of the Argens, and the chapel of Saint-Pierre-de-Baumont (the location of which is unknown), to Le Thoronet in lieu of rent. These probably became the centre of the granges. The abbey also probably owned a house on the Envessenes property, which was gradually incorporated into the abbey's holdings. Furthermore, the abbey held a number of seigneurial rights, which were collected in money or in kind from more distant properties. The system of direct ownership of the land, which was common for a time, was swept aside by the end of the thirteenth century. Later, the monastery acquired houses in the town, salt marshes and an expanse of grasslands and grazing rights for its animals along the coast and in Haute-Provence.

Lay brothers and *familiares*

Lay brothers already existed in the Cluny monasteries, but in the Cîteaux order, they were given an essential role in the financial organisation. These men (and there were often large numbers of them) were responsible for administering the property of the abbey both within the walls of the monastery and in more distant granges. The religious men came from a lower social class than the monks, who were frequently nobles. They were often illiterate and did not fully participate in the liturgical life of the Cistercians. They were distinguished from the monks by their beards. Other laymen were admitted alongside the lay brothers; they are referred to in texts as *familiares*. Little is known about these men, who were probably housed in the abbey. By the late thirteenth century, there were more *familiares* than lay brothers. In 1293, the general chapter decided to eliminate this class of residents, but it appears as though lay members—housekeepers and, later, farmers—always lived among the Cistercians.

The lay brothers can be identified by their brown robes and beards, hence their nickname, "the bearded brothers". Illumination from the manuscript of Garnier, abbot of Clairvaux in 1186. (Troyes, bibliothèque municipale).

Commendatory Abbots

In 1328, the abbot of Le Thoronet, supported by the inhabitants of nearby villages, accused his own monks of robbing the locals. Added to these problems were the wars and the Black Plague of 1348, which decimated the Provençal population. The villages were deserted, the land abandoned. Friction continued into the early fifteenth century. The arrival in 1416 of a *profès* * (professed monk) from Valsaintes to run the abbey was criticised by Antoine de Boniface, one of the twelve monks living at Le Thoronet, who accused the newcomer of simony* and

The terms followed by an asterisk are explained in the glossary at the end of the book.

Ruins in front of the lay brothers' building.

9

questioned the sincerity of his convictions. It seems clear that Mitre Gastinel, an influential figure at the court of King René, showed little concern for his abbey. His successor took over an establishment whose finances were in ruins and its buildings in a deplorable state.

In 1430, Griffin, who was an ecclesiastic and bishop of Ross in Scotland, but did not have an Episcopal see, was appointed governor of Le Thoronet by Pope Martin V. The abbot of Cîteaux protested this interference in the Cistercian organisation by a lay clergyman. In 1433, he entrusted Antoine de Boniface—a former monk at Le Thoronet who had become abbot of Silvacane—with the administration of the abbey and requested a report describing the ruined buildings, which housed only four monks at the time. This protest by the abbot of Cîteaux should be understood in the context of the commendatory system that was gaining ground throughout France. In the Middle Ages, the abbots came from the families of local nobles and were elected by the community of monks. In the fourteenth century, however, the popes in Avignon started claiming the right to appoint abbots themselves; by the fifteenth century, the king wanted to take over this privilege for political and financial reasons. The commendatory system achieved official status in 1516 through the concordat of Bologna, by which Pope Leo X granted François I the right to appoint those men who would receive ecclesiastical benefices. The position of abbot became a benefice granted to a dignitary who then administered the monastery and received a share of its income without having to reside on the premises.

Contemporary historians paint a fairly dismal portrait of the abbey from the sixteenth century on, but the situation may not have been so grim. The land was once again occupied, as the monastery granted parcels to farmers, who eventually acquired title to them. A series of commendatory abbots ran the monastery, with varying degrees of concern for the state of the buildings. The most solid structures—the cloister, dormitory, storeroom and building reserved for lay brothers—

According to local tradition, this statue represents Saint Laurence, but there is no trace of any of the saint's usual attributes.

This *Virgin and Child*, moved from Le Thoronet to the church at Lorgues, is attributed to the school of Pierre Puget, a 17th-century Provençal sculptor and architect.

were maintained, while other areas were sacrificed. By the late sixteenth century, during the Wars of Religion, it appears that the abbey was completely abandoned for a time. Ironically, the archives of Le Thoronet, transferred for safekeeping to the Château de Carcès during these wars, burnt there several years later. During the seventeenth century, a series of disagreements set the monks against their abbot, who refused to carry out the repairs they had requested. The abbey was then used as a parish church. Monks often left the monastery to administer sacraments, and women entered the cloisters to attend mass. The abbot offered to help the residents of Le Thoronet to build a church, and the priest of Lorgues was appointed as the parish priest in 1662.

In the eighteenth century, the initial Cistercian aesthetic, considered old-fashioned and unsuitable for prayer, was replaced by the more fashionable baroque. Abbeys throughout Europe were rebuilt in this new style. At Le Thoronet, Monsignor Phélipeaux, abbot from 1698 to 1751, limited the extent of the transformations to a "renovation" of his church, by adding stucco* in the shape of draperies, replastering the walls, and ordering woodwork and elaborate gilded metal gratings. The chancel windows were then transformed into alcoves to hold statues, including a *Virgin and Child* by the school of Pierre Puget, a *Saint Bernard* and a *Saint Laurence*. The latter sculpture was still in the cloister at the beginning of the twentieth century. According to local tradition, a young man who could roll the sculpture would wed within the year. This sculpture was moved to the dormitory; fortuitously, a head, which may or may not be the original, was found a few years ago and placed on the sculpture.

This same abbot was probably responsible for the famous avenue of chestnut trees to the south of the church. The various ponds in the nearby gardens, particularly the charming fountain at the end of the avenue, were created in the eighteenth century.

A clerk's report from the second half of the century describes a relatively luxurious lifestyle, in keeping with the life-style of the Cistercians of the period. A certain number of Cistercian monks had refused to follow the reforms proposed several years earlier by Abbot Rancé at the Trappe monastery. This reform would divide the order into two observances: the Cistercians of the Common Observance and the Order of Cistercians of the Strict Observance.

The community was deeply in debt, and in 1785, Monsignor de Flamarens—the last commendatory abbot and vicar-general of Bourges—signed a declaration of bankruptcy.

Following double page:

A section of wall to the south of the apse, still standing in 1952, indicated the location of the Lorgues gate, which was destroyed in 1874 when a local road was rerouted to run alongside the abbey. This road was moved away from the abbey in the 1960s.

The fountain among the chestnut trees, depicted soon after it was constructed in the late 18th century. This is one of the last architectural additions made by the monks. Ink drawing by Toulonnais artist Pierre Letuaire, 19th century (Société des Amis du Vieux Toulon).

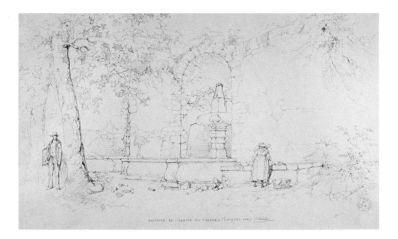

Secularisation and Privatisation

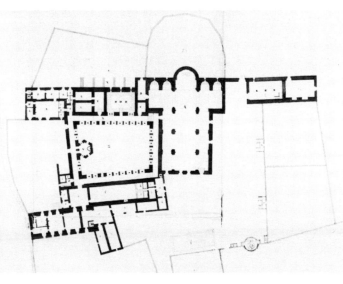

DE PAR LE ROI

FERME GÉNÉRALE DES REVENUS

DES MANSES ABBATIALE ET CONVENTUELLE
DE L'ABBAYE DE THORONET,
DIOCESE DE FRÉJUS, INDIVISES

The abbey's farmlands were leased out for the last time in 1786. The monks had long since stopped farming themselves (Draguignan, Archives départementales du Var).

This map, drawn up around 1791 by an architect from Toulon who signed it "Millou fils", is an invaluable record of the condition of the site, as it is the oldest and most detailed in existence. (Draguignan, Archives départementales du Var).

A decision was taken to deconsecrate Le Thoronet in 1785. It was placed under the king's responsibility, then rented out for a six-year lease to Jacques Clément Blond, an entrepreneur and salt-tax collector.

On 1 January 1791, the last seven monks remaining in the abbey were moved to other religious institutions. According to an announcement dated 28 May 1791, the abbey was to be sold as national property. The Republic's representative, however, had other views. The records of the sale indicate that they considered the cemetery, the long avenue of chestnut trees, the fountain and the church to be "treasures of art and architecture", which should therefore "remain the property of the Nation". This act, which occurred ninety-six years before Victor Hugo declared beauty to be "in the public interest" and one hundred twenty-two years before a law confirmed his belief, may be seen as one of the earliest attempts to classify a site as a historic monument.

The remainder of the property was sold on 17 March 1793. The new owners and the nearby townships used the stones from certain sections of the abbey as construction materials for their own buildings.

Reconstruction

The abbey was classified as a historical monument early on: it was included in the first list drawn up in 1840. A new chapter in the abbey's history began with a series of opposing restorations over the last one hundred fifty years aimed at re-creating the overall structure of the site. The work began in 1841 with the church and the bell tower. In 1845, Charles Auguste Questel (1807-1888), the chief architect for the *Monuments historiques*, drew up an architectural survey, which has become a precious source of information about the state of the monastery at that time. Some time later, the regional architect Lantouin restored the bell tower. He plastered the spire, which was made of rubble stone, but kept the small windows. By doing so, he triggered a debate concerning the authenticity of these windows; Prosper Mérimée, inspector general of the *Monuments historiques*, and others after him held that these openings were modern additions which should be eliminated.

In 1854, the State repurchased the cloister and its *lavabo**, the chapter-house, the courtyard and the dormitory. The architect Henri Révoil (1822-1900) took over from Questel. He removed the church's baroque decor, considered to be a perversion of the austerity extolled by Saint Bernard. Paradoxically, in 1874, he allowed a local road linking Lorgues to Cabasse to be rerouted alongside the south side of the abbey church, breaking the unity of the monastery.

The vaulted roof of the dormitory collapsed after a torrential rainfall in the autumn of 1906. It was rebuilt and reinforced with metal rods starting in 1907. Before he was appointed chief architect of the *Monuments historiques* in 1920, Jules Formigé (1879-

Very few examples of two-storey medieval cloisters remain, which explains why Viollet-le-Duc was so interested in Le Thoronet. He chose this site to illustrate the "cloisters" chapter in his *Dictionnaire raisonné de l'architecture française du XIᵉ au XVIᵉ siècle*. This watercolour cross-section by Questel (1845) also depicts the cloisters and the two superimposed galleries (Paris, Médiathèque du patrimoine).

The abbey seen from the west and from the north, by Médéric Mieusement, 1881, and from the north-east, anonymous photographer, 1865 (Paris, Médiathèque du patrimoine).

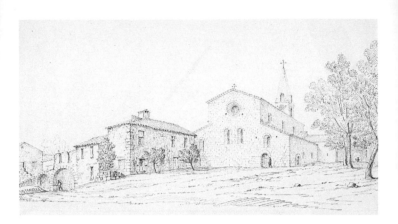

1960), assisted by François Roustan and his son, continued the renovation, basing the work on the nineteenth-century viewpoint which strived to create the idealised purity of the original architecture. In 1930, an overall plan to rehabilitate the abbey was drawn up. It called for filling in the four windows on the bell tower spire which, Formigé believed, were created in the eighteenth century. The cloister fountain was returned, and the cloister galleries, the sacristy, the chapter-house and the dormitory were restored one by one. The gate was reconstructed in 1939 from the considerable ruins still on the site. This reconstruction seems fairly similar to the medieval layout, but it destroyed precious information which modern archaeological methods would have been able to decipher. The work was recently completed by the restoration of an upper floor and a watchtower*, using a photograph taken in 1865.

The renovation stopped during World War II and began again with Formigé's successor, Paul Colas, in the 1950s. This work involved the outbuildings which had all become state

The abbey viewed from the west; drawing by Marseille architect Pascal Coste (1850). Buildings around the storeroom to the left, visible in this drawing, no longer exist (Marseille, Archives municipales).

A north-south sectional view of the lay brothers' building, drawn by Paul Colas in the 1960s, shows the latrines that straddled the Tombaréu stream. (Paris, Médiathèque du patrimoine).

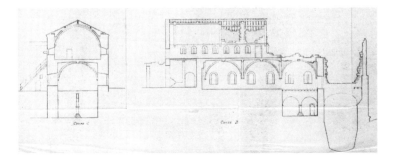

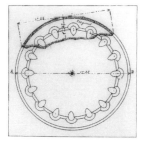

The *lavabo* in the cloister: upper basin reconstructed by François Roustan in 1924, and the *lavabo* pavilion, photographed in 1865 (Paris, Médiathèque du patrimoine).

The gate and watch-tower, photographed in 1865, and the watch-tower as reconstructed by Jules Formigé in 1932.

property. The local road was again rerouted to pass outside the monastery enclosure. Jean-Claude Ivan Yarmola, the chief architect in charge of the work at Le Thoronet from 1974 to his death in 1998, returned the bell tower to its original appearance; he also completed the restoration of the gate, to which he added a small gatehouse after an archaeological campaign was carried out. He dealt with serious destabilisation due to landslides; the abbey is still monitored constantly.

A bauxite deposit, mined from 1959 to 1989, is situated close to Le Thoronet. It was partially responsible for the destabilisation of

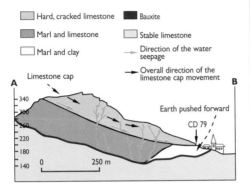

Hard, cracked limestone   Bauxite

Marl and limestone   Stable limestone

Marl and clay   Direction of the water seepage

   Overall direction of the limestone cap movement

Limestone cap

A   B

340
300
260
220
180
140

Earth pushed forward

CD 79

0   250 m

the valley subsoil which was serious enough to damage the walls of the abbey and dry up the valley springs. Explosions set off in the mine created cracks in the clay and marl on which rests the limestone cap at the top of the Darboussière hill. These soil masses became permeated by seepage water and by the underground water which had been contained by the limestone cap. The limestone then started to slip over the permeated subsoil at speeds varying from twenty-five centimetres to one metre per year, pushing the tithe* building towards the abbey church. The conclusion of a comprehensive survey proposed a costly and technically difficult solution to save the church. Vertical drains were dug to channel the underground water towards a large horizontal drainage gallery, several hundred metres long, which bypassed the abbey to the south. In 1984 and 1986, two series of core samples revealed that the abbey was not sitting on a rock foundation, but on an unstable mixture of limestone and bauxite. The underpinning of the building was stabilised by inserting a system of micropiles under the walls on the building's eastern side.

TOURING THE ABBEY

Within the Monastery Walls

According to the Rule of Saint Benedict, an abbey must be designed as an autonomous city. By choosing sites situated far from economic centres, the Cistercians applied this order to the letter. The working areas and those reserved for exchanges between the monks and the outside world were all situated within a thick wall. The monastic quarters, themselves organised around the cloister, were the centre of this city, and access to it was strictly forbidden to laymen.

The medieval layout of the enclosure surrounding Le Thoronet abbey is still largely unknown; there were, however, two gateways. The monumental twelfth-century gatehouse, aligned with the abbey church and surveyed by Formigé in 1932, had at least two storeys. There was also a gate for carts. The gatekeeper, who greeted guests and the sick, was housed on the upper floor. The

Postcard published around 1907 by Léopold Verger. The photograph was probably taken by the Séeberger brothers. Private collection.

Several sections of the enclosing wall in front of the olive grove.

other entrance, known as the Lorgues gate and located between the south transept of the nave and the grange, was destroyed when the local road was rerouted alongside the abbey in the nineteenth century.

According to Chapter XVI of Saint Benedict's Rule, the monastery should have "everything necessary—water, a mill, a garden, a bakery and dispensary—to conduct the various occupations, so that the monks have no need to roam outside, which is in no way beneficial to their souls". A few of the medieval structures linked to the material organisation of the abbey still exist at Le Thoronet. The grange was located in the southern corner of the enclosing wall, near the Lorgues gate. This structure, divided in half, is today known as the tithe grange. The northern half, with a groined vault* supported on three columns, was used as a stable in the late eighteenth century. At that time, an oil press occupied the other half. A medieval building with a lower barrel-vaulted room on transverse ribs* was unearthed to the north-west of the enclosure, where the Darboussière and Tombaréu streams come together. Historians believe it was a guest house, linked to the structures excavated near the gatehouse, and probably reserved for distinguished visitors. The flour mill and the bread oven mentioned in the fourteenth century have not yet been found.

There are few traces of the courtyard and gardens which existed around the monastery buildings in the sixteenth century, particularly around the axis connecting the gate and the church. The present-day gatehouse leads to a redesigned terraced garden; it has a central main basin and two small fountains discovered during the most recent archaeological excavations.

The double avenue of chestnut trees (farther to the east and south of the church), which had been described as early as 1791, was cut down in 1998 and replanted exactly as before, as the trees had grown too old. The avenue leads to a lovely sheltered eighteenth-century fountain with a semicircular basin fitted into a *cul-de-four,* * or quarter-sphere vault. It is tempting to believe that this is the

Long arch stones of an old door to the storeroom, visible behind a series of arches, reveal an earlier state of the building.

Situated to the north-west of the abbey, the double arches of this building—perhaps a guest house—were reconstructed to give an idea of how it must have appeared before the arched roof collapsed.

same fountain listed in the record books of 1778.

An interplay of water and light on the beautiful 18th-century fountain at the end of the avenue of chestnut trees, 1952.

The water comes from underground conduits which collect spring water farther to the south. A wall at right angles to the fountain runs along the row of chestnut trees. Several flights of stairs lead to gardens. Vines were probably planted in the sixteenth century to produce wine.

The tithe grange in 1962, divided by an internal wall.

Archaeology at Le Thoronet

Several archeological excavations have been conducted since 1986 by Michel Fixot, Jean-Pierre Pelletier and Caroline d'Annoville, particularly in the area around the gatehouse and the guest house. These structures fulfilled the requirements for hospitality and charity that was a part of the Rule, and were essential to the Cistercian organisation. Historians have recently established this fact, but traces of these structures are rare, and those that do exist have rarely been excavated.

The excavations first revealed that the site was occupied long before the Cistercians arrived in the twelfth century. An archaeological and historical hiatus preceded their establishment, demonstrated by the fifth- or sixth-century BC (or even earlier) hearth and kiln furnace unearthed to the south of the excavated area. These remains can be linked to other fortuitous discoveries (another potter's kiln, a bronze buckle plate*, sepulchres and so on), dated to the same period.

Foundations of buildings that appear to have been used for guests and remodelled several times during the thirteenth and fourteenth centuries have been unearthed to the south of the gate. A walkway, consisting of a corridor preceded by a covered porch, was created in the long rectangular room connected to the gatehouse; this room probably had an upper storey. Visitors entered the abbey by walking along the western wall; thus, they did not have to cross the Darboussière stream.

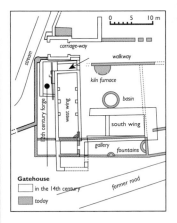

A building stood at right angles towards the east. It had very thick walls and was divided in half, at least on the ground level. Two small rooms were later added to the southeast. L-shaped galleries facing the courtyard ran alongside buildings. Although he cannot support his theory, Marcel Aubert, a specialist in Cistercian art, believes that the visitors' chapel—known in the fifteenth century and dedicated to Saint Catherine—was located somewhere nearby. It is impossible to confirm this hypothesis today.

A small forge existed on this site for a time before the footpath gate was created. A second furnace has been found slightly farther south; it was used to cast a bell. The monks tried to extract iron from the bauxite that was on their lands; these temporary installations were probably created during the abbey's construction.

The current gatehouse was constructed partially on these foundations.

Caroline d'Annoville

The Monastic Quarters

The abbey buildings, situated at the base of the Darboussière hill, followed the slope of the land. The church was located, as always, at the highest point of the site. The western facade has few windows and no buttresses*; it is one of the simplest that the order ever built. Like at Sénanque and Silvanès, another of Mazan's "daughters", there is no central door. This is because the church was reserved for monks, and a world of silence of prayer reigned within the monastic quarters. The heart of this area was the cloisters. Another characteristic of this facade no longer exists: it once followed the natural slope of the land; the ground in front of it has been raised up and levelled over the centuries, altering the original architectural balance. The medieval threshold of the left door, to the north, was much lower than it is today. The two side doors were thus both the same size. The north door was probably used by the lay members, who worked and sometimes lived outside of the monastery enclosure; the south door was reserved for the monks, funeral processions and the visiting dignitaries who, under special circumstances, were allowed into the church.

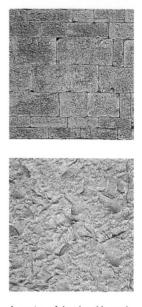

A section of the church's south wall carrying the gutters. The difficult job of sculpting the hard grey and pink limestone impressed architect Fernand Pouillon, who wrote *Les Pierres sauvages* (The Wild Stones), in which he re-creates the story of the abbey's construction.

Two narrow windows above the doors lead to the side aisles. The nave was lit by just two windows; above them is a simple oculus,* which matches the oculus on the church chevet.* As opposed to the western facades of secular churches, designed to welcome and edify believers, those on the Cistercian abbey churches had no particular decoration. The perfectly fitted stones in the semicircular apse, however, seem almost luxurious, as if to celebrate the glorious Parousia of Christ, who, one day, will return from the East.

To the south, the wall supporting the gutter adjoining the grange has two windows and a projecting alcove, built sometime after the initial construction. It is believed to be an *enfeu,** or recess for a tomb—the cemeteries in Cistercian abbeys were generally placed to the south of the church—or a more recent "depository", used as a temporary location

Following pages:

The semicircular apse was a common form in the Romanesque period.

The oculus and two windows of the west side of the church.

The dip in the ground in front of the church no longer exists. A recess* can be seen on the south wall.

for the remains of a parish member. At Le Thoronet, however, the only known medieval sepulchres were discovered to the east, near the chevet of the church, where the graveyard existed in 1791. The locations of the windows made in the eighteenth century are visible on the upper wall of the central

nave. To the east, the apse is framed by absidal chapels in a flat chevet. Historians are not certain whether the stone used for the construction was taken from a site east of the church. A document dated 1218 mentions an excessive supply of stones taken by the monks from the Cabasse property. Whatever the case, stones from another source were used for the top of the south wall, as well as for the western facade of the church.

The tiled roof rests directly on the arches and is finished with quarter-round coping stones. The bell tower consists of a square tower with small windows on which sits a pyramidal-shaped roof with recently restored windows having a *plein cintre,** or semicircular arched top. A statute dated 1157 recommends the construction of a single small bell, which could be easily rung by the sacristan, and forbade stone bell towers. Later, the general chapter altered this rule, as the increasing size of the abbeys required a more powerful sound that would reach the brothers working far from the resting and prayer buildings. A second, more modest bell tower and the use of stone were authorised during the thirteenth century, particularly to withstand the strong winds in southern France.

The Church Interior

The church offers a good example of the Cistercian aesthetic principles: it is oriented (arranged in relation to the points of the compass) and has three fairly wide naves crossed by a projecting transept. There are more straight and horizontal lines than curves, and the few decorative elements emphasise the essential design. The various construction stages can be detected through a few architectural changes made during construction, particularly in the use of different stone.

Several steps lead from the south door to the side aisle, then to the main nave, covered by a pointed barrel vault,* which continues to the intersection with the transept. The line of the vault is underscored by a horizontal course, a moulding that exists on almost every vault in the monastery. The transverse ribs—with a single curve and rectangular cross section—are supported by a cubic capital and then extended down the walls by engaged columns.* These half-columns, on which consecration crosses* are faintly visible, end at engaged bases.* These have a quarter-round shape at a certain height above the floor so that the wooden stalls can rest against the rectangular pillars punctuating the bays.* Healthy monks, the sick and the lay brothers were separated from each other during services; they each occupied one of three different choirs—or set of stalls. From single imposts,* the two curves of the archway continued upward via a flat engaged pilaster.* The side aisles, except in the north-east bay that has a half-barrel vault, are covered with a sloping barrel vault.* This is a common architectural feature in Provençal abbeys. The relatively low projecting transept intersects with the nave with two archways that are higher than those of the nave. The curves of the arches are supported by engaged columns resting on a pier that extends to the floor on the sanctuary side and rest on engaged piers on the nave side. The capitals framing the apse are decorated with crosses. The north wall of the transept has three windows. A small staircase leads down to the sacristy, and next to it, the matins* staircase leads up to the dormitory. Higher up, a window opens onto the sacristan's room. The transept is illuminated by a single window, with a semicircular arch, situated to the south. The four chapels in the transept, each illuminated by a semicircular-arched window, consist of a short pointed barrel-arched bay and a *cul-de-four* (quarter-sphere vault). Some of the eighteenth-century painting is still visible. The various types of courses used in the absidal chapels and the side aisles illustrate the trials and errors of the initial builders. Above the sanctuary is a triumphal wall* with a single oculus, supported by engaged columns. A pointed barrel-vaulted bay stands before the *cul-de-four* shaped apse. The apse has three windows—a traditional layout—with decorative insets that accentuate the play of light. A credence* and a semicircular alcove were built into the

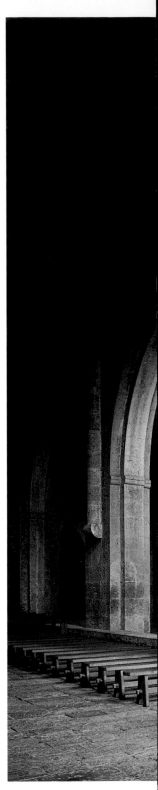

south wall. There is no piscina*; as at Sénanque, it must have been removable and
held in place by a hole in the floor.

Preceding pages:
Pillars in the nave and the
south aisle.

All the stained-glass windows in the abbey
were replaced by 1935; they were re-created
from the late original twelfth-century glass
stored in the Obazine abbey in Corrèze.
Plumb lines hanging from the top of the
church monitor any ground movement.

The play of light on the stone and acoustics
are essential factors in Cistercian spirituality.
Because stone was the only material used
and also because of the proportions, the
abbey churches of the White Monks were
perfectly adapted to the liturgical function of
the religious chants. At Le Thoronet, the Romanesque architects used their empirical
knowledge to work wonders, and the abbey
church remains famous for the quality of its
acoustics.

The Cloisters

This is the heart of the monastic complex.
The gardens and courtyards near the enclosing wall are charming, but the beauty of the
cloisters transfigures the entire abbey. It is
created by the rough, though perfectly

View of one of the chapels
opening on the transept.

The apse in quarter sphere vault of the abbey church choir. The Romanesque altar has been in the apse since the 12th century.

Following double page:

Le Corbusier was particularly inspired by Le Thoronet abbey, a complete example of the austere Cistercian style. According to the architect: "Light and shadow are the loudspeakers of this architecture of truth, calm and strength."

proportioned architecture, the large amount of natural stone that is integrated into the thick walls, and the reddish highlights from the bauxite contained in the stone.

This is one of the oldest remaining Cistercian cloisters and certainly the most austere. The floor plan is irregular, following the topography of the abbey. A few steps lead down from the north side aisle of the church to the south arcade of the cloisters, itself higher than the others. The arcades open onto the central courtyard via a series of semicircular arches divided in half by a large, squat column. A rough-cut capital supports two arches and a tympanum with an oculus. The bahut* is wide enough to withstand the thrust of the vault and to support the weight of the second-storey arcades (still visible in the nineteenth century) without requiring

buttressing. The north and west arcades, built later than the others, have several different decorative elements: groined vault and intersecting ribs, capitals sculpted with a leaf pattern, and a different string course cross-section. A tomb in the south-east corner, decorated with two semicircular arches supported by two small columns may have been designed by the legendary monk Guillaume de Florièges or the count of Provence, Alphonse II.

The southern arcade still has the original stone benches. A **porch**^M to the west was certainly used by the lay brothers to reach the church. The **lavabo**^K, opposite the abbey church, in front of the refectory entrance, stands at the edge of the courtyard. This small hexagonal room, whose roof is a ribbed vault* with six sections, has several doors. The fountain provided water for the monks' everyday use—washing up, shaving, tonsure and clothes-washing; it was reconstructed from a fragment of the upper central basin discovered in the early twentieth century. The spring water in the fountain crossed the cloisters from the lay brothers' porch and was discharged into the Tombaréu stream along with the kitchen waste water.

The Monks' Wing

The cloister's eastern arcade runs alongside the monks' building, which contained the same rooms as in all Cistercian monasteries: sacristy, library, chapter-house, dormitory staircase, passage and/or locutory and the monks' hall. In this building, the **sacristy**^C can only be reached from the church. Although it was built after the transept, it has the same width. The north wall has several alcoves. The first vaulted room has a semicircular arch and faces the cloisters. This was the library, or *armarium*^D. Above the double bay is a cubic capital and a saddleback* lintel supported by moulded imposts. The rabbets meant to hold the wooden shutters in the library are still visible on the central column.

The next room is the **chapter-house**^E, or hall, where the monks met every morning to read

Collection of translations by Denis l'Aréopagite, 12th-century manuscript. A 14th- or 15th-century annotation indicates that it belonged to the *armarium* of Le Thoronet (Carpentras, bibliothèque Inguimbertine).

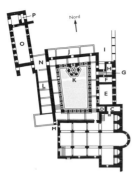

The *lavabo* pavilion and the fountain.

The door of the *armarium*, which housed the books used by the monks for their personal meditations. The liturgical books were kept in the sacristy.

a chapter from the Benedictine Rule or other religious works. Several steps lead down to this smaller space, designed according to a traditional layout: the ground is lower than the arcades of the cloisters, there is a predetermined number of windows, a vault on intersecting ribs supported by central columns, and tiers for seating. The six intersecting ribbed vaults are supported in the centre by two massive columns, and against the walls by engaged bases. A six-petal flower decorated the keystone. The column capitals are decorated with a few figurative elements among the flat sculpted leaves, called "water leaves": pine cones, palm leaves, flowers, a hand holding a crosier, a cross and a heart-shaped design.

The monks sat on wooden tiers built into the rocky outcrops. In this century, stone steps have been reconstructed in half of the room. The abbot sat facing the door, where an altar would later stand. There are three windows to the east. Towards the cloisters, two semicircular arches, divided into three sections by small twinned columns, frame the entrance door. A vaulted **passageway**[F], or corridor, connects the cloisters with the monks' garden to the east. Next is the **staircase**[G], leading to the dormitory, and farther along, a **small room**[H], which has been remodelled several times; it may have been used as a locutory, office or archive room. The last door, which no longer opens, led to a building which no longer exists, but which must have contained the **monks' hall**[I]. This is where the monks worked in winter and when occupied with more meticulous tasks; novices also may have received instruction in this room. By the sixteenth century, this area was restructured. As the north wing was in ruins, the refectory was transferred to this site in the eighteenth century. No architectural analysis has ever been made of the few elements visible on the outside—including a series of arcades. The dormitory occupied the upper storey of the eastern wing. The pointed barrel-vault—originally made of tuff, as discovered by Jean-Claude Ivan Yarmola—partially collapsed in 1906. It was reconstructed in hard limestone and

41

stabilised using reinforcing bars. The transverse ribs rest on simple quarter-round engaged bases. Some of the small windows to the east were enlarged in recent years.

The floor was covered with stone slabs and terracotta tiles that repeated the design of the pacing stones found on the site around 1920, but which have since been lost. In the sixteenth century, doors were made in the east side of the building, leading to terraces resting on the buttresses. The dormitory probably extended to the north, perhaps with a dormitory for novices and by the latrines. Doors to the west led to the upper cloisters. In the seventeenth century, individual cells were made here and in the dormitory. Another door to the west led to the abbot's room, constructed on the cloisters at the same time as the dormitory. Historians are uncertain about the function of a rectangular mass constructed opposite, on the sacristy. It may have housed the archives or the relics, or it may have been the room of the sacristan, who watched over the church and woke up the monks for night mass by ringing the dormitory bell from his bed. A modern bell since has been restored on the outside of the building, at the top of the transept gable.

Detail of the pine-cone decoration sculpted on one of the capitals in the chapter-house.

The chapter-house opened out onto the cloister gallery.

The North Wing

Three doors (now closed off) in the north wall of the north arcade led to the rooms that were traditionally located opposite the church: the calefactory*, the refectory and the kitchens. This entire wing has disappeared. The original **refectory** had a barrel-vaulted roof and was divided into several rooms and a mezzanine sometime after it was first constructed. The building was abandoned by 1791, but a staircase leading to the upper storey still existed. A courtyard to the north stood around a circular basin.

One of the central columns in the chapter-house that supports the ribbed vaults and transverse ribs— one of the few architectural components with decorative elements.

The dormitory.

The Storeroom

According to the Benedictine layout, the **storeroom**^L occupied the western wing of the cloisters, as well as the refectory and the dormitory for the lay members. The lay brothers' building and the storeroom were located in two separate buildings at Le Thoronet. A door in the north-west corner of the cloisters led to a **small courtyard**^N; the south end was formed by the storeroom and the west end by the lay members' building and a covered passageway. The original layout of the storeroom, which has been altered several times over the centuries, is still difficult to determine. The west wall, for example, still shows where a wide door and loopholes, visible from the outside, once existed. These openings, once erroneously considered to be part of a building that predates the abbey, were closed off by a series of arches that reinforced the wall during the construction of the barrel vault.* The locations of several other doors from different periods are also visible in the cloister's west arcade. The building probably extended farther to the north. The southern section—transformed into a guest house and a caretaker's home, and today the site's administrative offices—seems to be independent of the large pointed barrel-vaulted room. Modern fermentation and grape-crushing tanks were kept in the storeroom, as the monks produced wine in the abbey from the sixteenth century on. The external side of the storeroom's western wall is lined with the ruins of a porch. The map drawn up in 1791 places the stables and a staircase leading to the upper storey somewhere in this vicinity.

A small courtyard linking the cloisters, the storeroom and the lay brothers' building.

The Lay Members' Building

The ground dipped so far to the north of the abbey that the **lay members' building°** had to be constructed on a lower room reached by a staircase placed against the eastern facade. The refectory, on the ground floor, consisted of a single vaulted hall with segmental pointed arches resting on simple engaged bases. The small medieval loopholes were enlarged in the eighteenth century. Only two of the bays have been restored. An exterior staircase led to the upper storey. The hall once housed the lay brothers' dormitory; it has a pointed barrel-vault and transverse ribs supported by large bases. The loophole windows were re-created from the window frames found on the site. To the north, three arches of the building straddle the Tombaréu stream; the **latrines°** were located here. In the eighteenth century, the building was transformed into the abbot's accommodations.

The refectory of the lay brothers' building in 1952.

Chronology

1098 The Cistercian order is founded.

1113-1245 The local Catalan counts rule Provence.

1136 Notre-Dame-de-Florièges abbey is founded.

1140 Raimond and Étiennette des Baux donate salt marshes and pastures.

1142-1162 The rulers of Les Baux wage war against the Catalan counts of Provence.

1147 The count of Provence, Raymond Béranger II, confirms the abbey property.

Before 1157 The community moves from Florièges to Le Thoronet.

1176 The count of Provence, Alphonse I, confirms the abbey property.

Before 1205 The troubadour Folquet de Marseille is elected abbot of Le Thoronet.

1246-1481 Provence comes under the rule of the Anjou counts of Provence.

1348 The Black Plague strikes the region.

1430 Bishop Griffon is appointed head of Le Thoronet by the pope.

1487 Provence becomes part of France.

1516 Concordat of Bologna: Pope Leo X grants French King François I the right to appoint commendatory abbots.

1577 An inventory is made of the abbey property during the Wars of Religion.

1614 Probable disappearance of some of the abbey's archives in a fire at the Château de Carcès.

1666 Pope Alexander VII approves the two Cistercian observances: the Cistercians of the Common Observance and the Order of Cistercians of the Strict Observance; the latter called for a return to the original asceticism of the order.

1698 Monsignor Phélipeaux is named abbot of Le Thoronet and renovates the abbey church.

1785 The abbey is declared bankrupt and is secularised.

1791 The sale of part of the abbey property as national property is announced.

1840 The abbey is one of the first structures to be classified a historical monument.

1841 Restoration work begins.

1854 The government purchases the cloisters and the monks' quarters.

1938 The government acquires the rest of the abbey: the storeroom, the lay brothers' building and, after World War II, the tithe grange.

1978 The sisters of Bethlehem install an exhibition hall and an oratory in the lay members' building.

1988 The foundations are stabilised to save the abbey, which had been threatened by major landslides.

Glossary

Bahut: a low wall; used in cloisters to designate the wall which supports the roof separating the galleries of the courtyard.

Barrel vault: a vault having a uniform section, in the form of a semicircular arch.

Bay: division of a nave, defined by four supporting members. In a directionally situated church, the bays are counted from west to east.

Buckle plate: an element of clothing in the Middle Ages, consisting of a buckle attached to a worked metal or ivory plate.

Buttress: external masonry element supporting a wall.

Calefactory: heated sitting room in a monastery.

Chevet: the rounded end of a church choir, including the apse and the aisles around it.

Commendam: a benefice held by a cleric, not usually a member of the regular order, who is named abbot by the pope or the king.

Consecration (cross of): twelve crosses were painted on the walls of the nave during the dedication or consecration services held for a new church, over which the bishop presided.

Credence: a table on which the church vessels and burettes for the mass are kept.

Cul-de-four (vault): a half-dome or quarter sphere vault.

Enfeu: recess for a tomb.

Engaged base: support embedded in a wall.

Engaged column: a pilaster-like element built as part of the wall.

Groined vault: vault formed of four sections that intersect; these intersecting angles are sometimes hidden by arches.

Impost: uppermost part of an abutment, part from which an arch springs.

Lavabo: the fountain in a cloisters.

Matins: evening prayer, also called vigils, and by extension, the name given to the staircase used by the monks to walk from their sleeping quarters to the church at night.

Oculus: a bull's eye window.

Pilaster: an engaged pier projecting slightly from a wall.

Piscina: an alcove near the altar holding a basin with a drain; the water used for ablutions and for purifying sacred vessels is poured into it.

Plein ceintre: a semicircular arch.

Pointed barrel vault: a barrel vault with a pointed cross-section.

Profès (professed): said of a person who has just taken vows in a religious order.

Recess: alcove in the wall of a church in which tombs are placed.

Ribbed vault: vault supported by at least two diagonal ribs, called groins, and two transverse arches.

Saddleback: used to designate an element that slopes equally on either side from a roof ridge.

Simony: act of purchasing or selling sacred or ecclesiastic benefices.

Sloping barrel vault: arch with an asymmetrical form.

Stucco: decor made of plaster of Paris.

Tithe: a tax imposed by the church on the annual crop production and herds of animals.

Transverse rib: called *arc doubleau* in French architecture, signifying a moulded arch supporting the vault.

Triumphal wall: wall with an archway over it, located at the entrance to the sanctuary of the crossing of the transept.

Watch-tower: angle turret or tower corbelled out from a curtain wall or angle.

A short bibliography

Aubert (Marcel), « Abbaye de Thoronet », *Congrès archéologique de France, Aix-en-Provence et Nice*, 1932, Paris, 1933, pp. 224-243.

Barbier (Edmond-Fernand), « Le Thoronet, forêt, pierres et cigales », *Dossiers d'archéologie*, n° 234, June-July 1998, pp. 120-123.

Id., *L'Abbaye cistercienne du Thoronet au Moyen Âge. Son origine, son territoire, ses possessions*, Marguerittes, Équinoxe, coll. « Mémoires du Sud », 1994.

Dimier (Anselme), *L'Art cistercien*, La Pierre-qui-Vire, Zodiaque, 1962.

Duby (Georges), *Saint Bernard. L'Art cistercien*, Paris, Flammarion, coll. « Champs », 1979.

Fixot (Michel), d'Annoville (Caroline), Molina (Nathalie) et Pelletier (Jean-Pierre), « Porteries et bâtiments d'accueil cisterciens : Silvacane et Le Thoronet », *Dossiers d'archéologie*, n° 229, December 1997-January 1998, pp. 108-111.

Kinder (Terryl N.), *L'Europe cistercienne*, La Pierre-qui-Vire, Zodiaque, 1997.

Pacaut (Marcel), *Les Moines blancs. Histoire de l'ordre de Cîteaux*, Paris, Fayard, 1993.

Pouillon (Fernand), *Les Pierres sauvages*, Paris, Seuil, 1964.

Pressouyre (Léon), *Le Rêve cistercien*, Paris, Gallimard/CNMHS, coll. « Découvertes », 1992.

Pressouyre (Léon) et Kinder (Terryl N.), dir., *Saint Bernard et le monde cistercien*, Paris, CNMHS, 1990, new edition 1992.

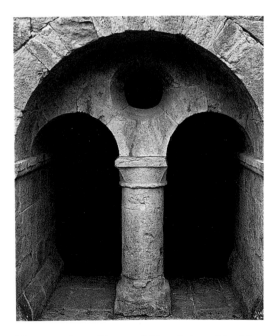

The warm colours of the stone brighten the bays of the cloister.